FLOWER & BIRD

Adult Coloring Book

Published by EMMA MIA in 2016

First edition: First printing

Illustrations and design © 2016 EMMA MIA

Author Contact

Group Facebook "**Best Book By EMMA MIA**"

www.fb.com/groups/1523056898003358/

ISBN-13: 978-1541231115

ISBN-10: 1541231112

Gifts

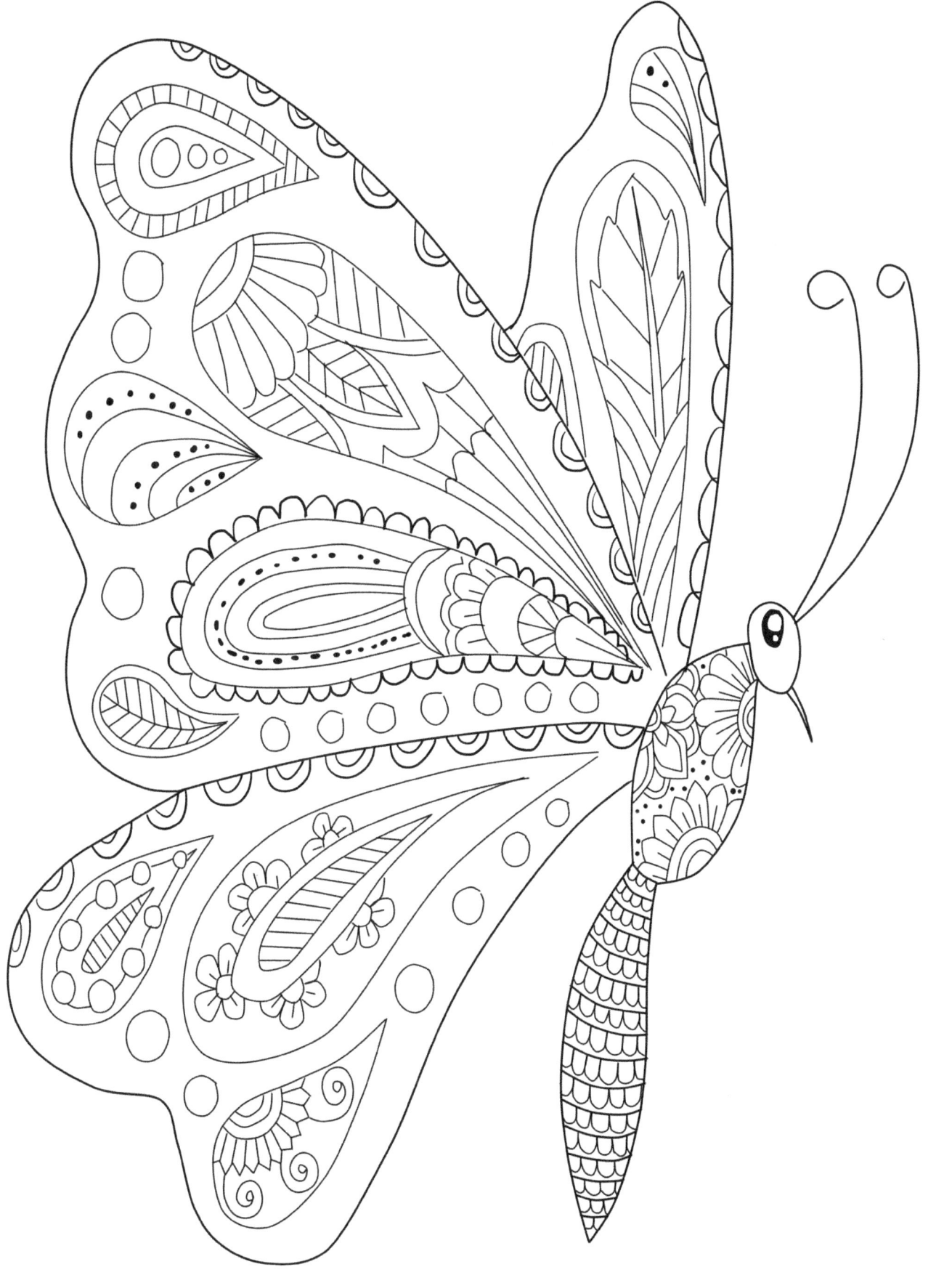

www.ingramcontent.com/pod-product-compliance
Lightning Source LLC
Chambersburg PA
CBHW081854280526
45789CB00007B/2697